ALL-TIME GUT-BUSTING FAVORITES

Why don't blondes eat bananas?
They can't find the zipper.

What was the last thing Nicole Simpson said?
"I should have had a V-8."

Why are there so few Polish monks?
The vow of silence includes farting.

How did Helen Keller burn the side of her face?
She answered the iron.

What do you call five lepers in a hot tub?
Soup.

GROSS JOKES

by Julius Alvin

AWESOMELY GROSS JOKES	(0-8217-3613-2, $3.50)
AGONIZINGLY GROSS JOKES	(0-8217-3648-5, $3.50)
INTENSELY GROSS JOKES	(0-8217-4168-3, $3.50)
INFINITELY GROSS JOKES	(0-8217-4785-1, $3.99)
TERRIBLY GROSS JOKES	(0-8217-4873-4, $3.50)
SAVAGELY GROSS JOKES	(0-8217-5149-2, $4.50)

THE BEST OF GROSS JOKES: VOLUME I

Julius Alvin

Zebra Books
Kensington Publishing Corp.
http://www.zebrabooks.com

ZEBRA BOOKS are published by

Kensington Publishing Corp.
850 Third Avenue
New York, NY 10022

First Printing: November, 1996
10 9 8 7 6 5 4 3 2

Printed in the United States of America

Contents

THE BEST GROSS RACIAL AND ETHNIC JOKES

What do Klu Klux Klan members do before they play cards?
Take out all the spades and burn them.

Did you hear the Russians are remodeling Chernobyl?
They're turning it into a synagogue.

Did you hear about the Puerto Rican who didn't know the difference between arson and incest?
He set his sister on fire.

How does a WASP housewife know dinner is ready?
The smoke alarm goes off.

Why are the sturdiest chairs made out of kosher wood?
They never tip.

Why did the Polish housewife serve curry with baked beans?
She loved Indian music.

Did you hear about the Polack who stayed up all night trying to figure out where the sun went when it set?
It finally dawned on him.

Did you hear about the guy who ran into a Puerto Rican bar and yelled "Fire!"
Everyone did.

Why did it take the Polish couple a week to drive from New York to Boston?
They kept seeing signs that read, "Clean rest room."

Why was the wheelbarrow invented in Africa?
So blacks could learn to walk on their hind legs.

Why was the Polish wife mad at her husband?
Because he was off shooting craps and she didn't know how to cook them.

Did you hear about the black man who suffered from insomnia?
He kept waking up every few days.

What's Poland's solution to the oil crisis?
Import a million tons of Arabian sand and dig their own wells.

A WASP husband was humping his wife when suddenly, to his surprise, she wiggled and let out a short cry of delight.

"My God, honey!" he exclaimed. "What happened?"

"It's wonderful," she said. "I finally decided that those curtains would look better in peach."

———

What's the definition of a macho WASP?
One who jogs home from his vasectomy.

———

How did the Polish mother finally stop her kid from biting his nails?
She made him wear shoes.

———

Why did the Italian Army form an attack force consisting solely of epileptics?
So the enemy couldn't tell which ones had been shot.

———

How do you break a Polack's finger?
Punch him in the nose.

What's the first thing a Russian woman has to do before she takes a bath?
Grease the sides of the tub so she doesn't stick.

What do they call the brother of an Italian mother?
A monkey's uncle.

What do you call an Italian woman?
A pizza ass.

Why did the Italian salesman quit his new job?
The boss gave him a virgin territory.

What do the Post Office and the Kinney Shoe Company have in common?
500,000 black loafers.

Why don't more black women become nuns?
Because they can't remember to say "Superior" after "Mother."

What's the definition of a black genius?
A man who can name his own children.

"My wife is a typical WASP," the man complained to his friend on the train to Connecticut. "She'll only make love doggie style."

"Doggie style? I don't believe it," his friend said.

"Yeah. I sit up and beg, then she rolls over and plays dead."

Where's the safest place to hide money from your black housekeeper?
Under the soap.

What's a black virgin?
An ugly first grader.

How can you tell a Polish woman is having her period?
She's only wearing one sock.

What's the most sought after rank in the Greek navy?
Rear admiral.

How did the Polish entrepreneur become a millionaire?
He took a plane to America, bought 100,000 metal coat hangers, took them back to Poland, and sold them as home abortion kits.

What's the definition of frenzy?
An Italian with a credit card in a whorehouse.

Two Polacks walked into a bar. The bartender asked, "What has four legs and stinks?"

"I don't know," one replied.

"You and your friend," the bartender said.

Later, the two Polacks were walking down the street when they spotted two friends. One Polack said to them, "What has four legs and stinks?"

The two men said they didn't know.

The Polack replied, "Me and my friend."

What's the definition of a redneck?
A guy who'll screw a black girl but won't go to school with her.

Why is a tampon like a Jewish American Princess?
They're both stuck up cunts.

What does a football and a Polish girl have in common?
Pigskin.

How do Italian girls protect themselves from peeping toms?
They keep the curtains open.

What's the definition of an erection on a Polack?
A ski lift.

What's the difference between a Jew and an Italian?
The Jew's the one in the Italian suit.

What do they call the Polish edition of *Who's Who?*
What's That?

Why couldn't the Italian man buy his wife a mink coat?
The fur clashed with her mustache.

What's the most effective birth control device for an Italian woman?
Her face.

Why did God give Italians arms?
So their fingers don't smell like their armpits.

How did the Jewish mother lose 20 pounds?
She washed off her make-up.

Why do Arab women wear veils?
So they can blow their noses without getting their hands dirty.

Why is the camel called the "ship of the desert?"
Because it's filled with Arab semen.

———

What color is a Negro who's been run over by a steam-roller?
Flat black.

———

What does NAACP stand for?
Niggers Are Actually Colored Polacks.

———

What's the definition of nigger?
A Negro who just left the room.

———

How do they make Italian sausage?
From retarded pigs.

———

How do you tell a WASP family at a Chinese restaurant?
They're the ones that aren't sharing.

Why couldn't the Polack be buried at sea?
The funeral director drowned trying to dig the grave.

How do Arabs make shish kebob?
They shoot an arrow into a rotting camel.

Why don't blacks ever drown?
Their lips are built-in inner tubes.

What's the definition of a black loser?
One who doesn't have the carfare to get to the welfare office.

What do products manufactured in Puerto Rico have imprinted on them?
"Untouched by human hands."

Why did the aquarium in Warsaw close?
The clams died.

What's the difference between an Irish wedding and an Irish funeral?
One less drunk.

What do they call a stork that delivers babies in Harlem?
A dope peddler.

What's the most common Polish marriage proposal?
"You're gonna have a what?"

How do Polacks reproduce?
They exchange underwear.

Why did the birth rate in Russia go up so dramatically?
The waiting list to have an abortion got to be ten months long.

How do you brainwash an Italian?
Step on his enema bag.

Why did the fisherman marry a Mexican woman?
She had a fine crop of worms.

Why don't people in Poland believe in reincarnation?
Who wants to die and come back a Polack?

What's the main advantage to being black?
You never miss an important call because you're in the bathtub.

Do all Polish teachers have ESP?
Yes—Extra Simple Pupils.

How can you tell a Polish pencil?
It has an eraser at both ends.

How can you cut the Puerto Rican birth rate by 75 percent?
Eliminate conjugal visits.

What's one advantage of being a redneck?
You and your wife's family reunion are the same event.

If Tarzan and Jane were Irish, what would Cheetah be?
The designated driver.

What did they find when they tore down the Berlin Wall?
The hide-and-seek champion of Poland.

Why don't Poles jerk off in the shower?
They don't want to see their kids go down the drain.

How can you recognize a Polish helicopter?
It's the one with the ejection seat.

Did you hear about the Polack who opened a Cajun restaurant?
The house speciality was blackened toast.

How can you tell a pirate is Polish?
He's got a patch over both eyes.

What's the first prize in the Polish lottery?
Ten dollars a year for a million years.

Where can you buy panties made out of fertilizer sacks and bras made out of beer cans?
Frederick's of Poland.

Why did the redneck die in the pie-eating contest?
The cow stepped on his head.

What's the difference between an Iranian terrorist and a JAP?
An Iranian terrorist makes fewer demands.

Did you hear about the new inflatable JAP doll?
You put a ring on its finger and its hips expand.

Why do Jewish men die before their wives?
They want to.

Why is a Jewish divorce so expensive?
Because it's worth it.

"Hey, ma," the kid called out as he came in the front door. "I found out today that I have the longest pecker in the third grade."

"That's great," his mother said.

"Is it because I'm black, Ma?" the kid asked.

"No," his mother replied, "It's because you're fourteen."

What do you call a black woman with two or more daughters?
Madam.

What do you call a black woman who's had an abortion?
A crime fighter.

What do you call the new cereal for black men?
"Nuttin' Bitch."

What do you call a hookers' convention?
The Miss Black America competition.

What do you call a black member of the G.O.P?
A Republi-coon.

What do you call a housing project in Harlem?
A coon-diminium.

Why do they let Puerto Ricans in the Army?
So the blacks have somebody to look down on.

Why don't Italians barbecue?
The spaghetti keeps falling through the grill.

What do you call a night with a JAP who has a yeast infection?
A whine and cheese party.

Why is an aspirin white?
You want it to work, don't you?

What's the difference between an African-American and shit?
After a while, shit turns white and stops stinking.

How do you rape a black woman?
Don't pay her.

What does NRA really stand for?
"Nigger Removal Agency."

Did you hear about the new Mexican sports car?
It's got four on the floor—and twelve in the backseat.

———

Why did the Polack stick his prick in boiling water?
His wife told him to go get sterilized.

———

Why couldn't the Irishman finish his drinking song?
He could never get past the first few bars.

———

A guy walked into a bar and saw his Italian friend downing double after double. He sat down next to him and asked, "Angelo, what's wrong?"

Angelo grimaced. "I got problems with my mother-in-law."

"Relax. Everyone's got problems with their mothers-in-law."

"Yeah," Angelo admitted. "But not everybody gets them pregnant."

Did you hear about the Polish inventor who crossed a toaster and an electric blanket?
It's for people who want to pop out of bed.

———

How can you tell if an Italian guy's in the Mafia?
His favorite dish is broken leg of lamb.

———

How can you tell a WASP household?
Their *TV Guide* is in hardcover.

———

Did you hear about the Puerto Rican burglar?
He got so successful he stopped making housecalls.

———

How can you tell if a WASP is a talented lover?
Last time he fucked his wife, she lost her place in her book twice.

The Polish guy walked into his bedroom and saw his wife sitting on the floor with her legs spread, naked, staring at her cunt. "What are you doing?" he asked.

She replied, "Studying for my Pap tests."

Who always drives the hottest cars?
Puerto Ricans—everything they drive is stolen.

How can you tell if a guy is Polish?
Every time he walks into an elevator, the operator says, "Basement."

What's the difference between a young French girl and a young Polish girl?
A young French girl turns heads; a young Polish girl turns stomachs.

What card do all Jewish mothers carry in their wallet?
One that reads, "In case of accident, I'm not surprised."

How dumb are Polacks?
Even their wisdom teeth are retarded.

Why don't Jews drink?
It interferes with their suffering.

Did you hear about the Polish guy who went on *The Dating Game?*
He chose himself—and scored.

What's the difference between an Irishman and a Muslim?
An Irishman gets stoned before he sleeps with someone else's wife.

Why did the sign outside the Polish swimming club read "OOL?"
They didn't want any "P" in it.

———

How can you tell a black kid has been crying?
His face is clean.

———

What's an Italian three-piece combo?
An organ, a cup, and a monkey.

———

What's the most common decoration in the Italian Army?
The Yellow Heart.

Two Polacks met on the street and one said, "I heard your brother died. What happened?"

"It was very sad," the other replied. "Lettuce killed him."

"How could lettuce kill a man?"

"This way," the Polack replied. "He bought lettuce at the market and asked the store owner how to keep it fresh. The owner told him, 'Put your head in a plastic bag, tie it tight, and put it in the refrigerator.' "

———

The black kid had been in his new school for just two days when he came home and said, "Ma, my teacher say I gotta take a bath or I can't go back. I got B.O."

Mama got furious, grabbed her pocketbook and her son's hand, and stormed off to school. She barged into the teacher's room, bellied her 250 pounds up to the desk, and shouted, "My Rufus ain't no pussy—you're supposed to learn him, not smell him."

———

A 13-year-old black girl came into class an hour late and the teacher asked, "Why are you so late?"

The girl said, "I be late because my brother needed me."

The teacher asked, "Couldn't he have done what he had to do by himself?"

"I don't think so," Crystal said. "He was fucking me."

The JAP whined to her husband, "Why won't you buy me a mink coat? I'm always so very, very, very cold."

Her husband replied, "If you already know the answer, why ask the question?"

Why shouldn't you feel sorry for Puerto Rican babies who are unwanted?
By the time they're fourteen, they'll be wanted in a dozen states.

What's so unique about redneck hospitals?
The maternity ward has a bridal suite.

What's the biggest Christian dilemma?
If Jesus was Jewish, how come he's got a Puerto Rican name?

Did you hear about the Irish woman whose doctor told her not to touch anything alcoholic?
She threw her husband out of the house.

How can you tell an Irishman in a fancy French restaurant?
He's trying to decide what wine goes best with whiskey.

———

How do you know you've moved into the wrong neighborhood?
You take your kid to school and a guy in a suit says, "I be da principal."

———

Why are Harlem gang members like Santa Claus?
Every night they go for a slay ride.

———

What should you do if you see a Polack walk into a restaurant with a beautiful woman on his arm?
Ask where he got the tattoo.

———

Did you hear about the four Irish guys who went on a hunting trip?
In four days, they killed 20 bottles of whiskey.

How do Polish kids learn to put on their underwear?
"Yellow in front, brown behind."

What do Puerto Ricans exchange instead of wedding rings?
Flea collars.

How can you tell if an Italian guy is homesick for his wife?
He's in the bedroom beating off into a Brillo pad.

What's the first thing a white girl does if she thinks she's in labor?
Finds out how far it is to the nearest hospital.

What's the first thing a black girl does if she thinks she's in labor?
Finds out how far it is to the nearest dumpster.

What do you know happened when you see an oil slick in the ocean?
Either an Exxon tanker crashed or four Italian guys went swimming.

What do you call ten canaries behind a curtain?
A Polish peep show.

What's a Polish burglar alarm?
Teaching the kids to bark.

What do you call a Mexican with herpes?
Manny Sores.

What do you get when you cross a black and an Indian?
A Sioux named Boy.

Why did the Polack cut his nose apart?
To see how it ran.

What do you call a Mexican with a vasectomy?
A dry Martinez.

What do Polish men do when their wives have their periods?
Give them a sock in the puss.

What's a Super Bowl to a Polack?
One that doesn't back up.

How do you execute a Mexican?
Sit him in wet cement, let it harden, then wait until it explodes.

Why did the Mexican eat refried beans?
To get a second wind.

Why did the Polack throw away his toilet brush?
He went back to using paper.

What did the Polack do after his girlfriend told him picking his nose was disgusting?
He picked it himself.

What's the difference between a JAP and jello?
Jello moves when you eat it.

———

What's the difference between courting a JAP and marrying a JAP?
When you court a JAP, she plays hard to get; when you marry her, she's impossible to get.

———

How long do rednecks cook their meat?
Until the tire marks disappear.

———

Where does a redneck go for food?
Highway 101.

———

Why don't they cremate Irishmen?
Last time they tried, it took a week to put out the fire.

———

How can you tell an Irishman in a topless bar?
He's there to drink.

Why is a porno movie like an Irish bar?
They're both full of guys getting stiff.

Did you hear about the religious Irish wife?
She wouldn't screw during any week that had a Sunday in it.

The Italian woman ran into a friend at the market and said, "Did you hear that Sophia got married?"

"No!" the other woman exclaimed. "I didn't even know she was pregnant."

What's the difference between a Polish girl and garbage?
Garbage eventually gets picked up.

Why isn't there any prostitution in Poland?
Polish woman can't even give it away.

What did the Polack do when a bee stung him on the cock?
Asked the doctor to take away the pain but leave the swelling.

How can you tell an Irishman at an orgy?
He's the one saying "My turn again?"

What do you call a woman in Israel who will fuck and suck all night?
A tourist.

What do you call an Irish couple who use the rhythm method of birth control?
Parents.

The young Polish couple was at the doctor's for their prenuptial physicals. At the end, the doctor called in the prospective groom and said, "I've got some good news and some bad news."

The young man grimaced. "What's the bad news?"

"Your fiancée has syphilis."

"Oh, no!" he cried. "What could possibly be the good news?"

"She didn't get it from you."

How do we know Adam was Irish?
Who else would have stood next to a naked woman and munched on an apple?

What did the Irishman say when he saw his best friend on top of his wife?
"Down, Rover."

Why aren't there any Irish bisexuals?
Twice a year is too much for them.

What's an Irish porno film?
Sixty seconds of sex and fifty-nine minutes of whiskey commercials.

Why do hookers like turning a trick with an Irishman?
It's a soft job.

Why are Irish men like bumper stickers?
They're hard to get off.

How do we know rednecks are lazy?
They all marry pregnant women.

Why is a JAP like a prizefighter?
She won't go into action until she sees a ring.

Why did the Irish newlyweds stay up all night?
They were waiting for their sexual relations to arrive.

What was the name of the Irish nymphomaniac?
Tramp O'Leen.

What do you call a JAP's waterbed?
Lake Placid.

What's another name for a JAP's waterbed?
The Dead Sea.

What's the first thing a JAP bride does?
Signs up for headache lessons.

How do you get a one-armed Polack out of a tree?
Wave to him.

How do you drive a Polack crazy?
Give her a bag of M&Ms and tell her to alphabetize them.

How do you know when a Polack has been making chocolate chip cookies?
You find M&M shells all over the kitchen floor.

What job does a Polack do in an M&M factory?
Proofreading.

Do you know why the Polack got fired from the M&M factory?
For throwing out the "W"s.

How did the Polack try to kill the bird?
She threw it off a cliff.

———

How did the Polack break her leg raking leaves?
She fell out of the tree.

———

How did the Polack die drinking milk?
The cow fell on her.

———

How did the Polack burn her nose?
Bobbing for french fries.

———

How can you tell when a FAX is from a Polack?
There is a stamp on it.

———

Why did the Polish woman only change her baby's diapers every month?
Because the package says they're "good for up to 20 pounds."

What did the little Jewish lady say to the flasher after he exposed himself?
"You call that a lining?"

Why do Jewish men watch porno movies backwards?
They love seeing the hooker hand the money back.

Exactly how much did the JAP hate sex?
She even had her guppies fixed.

Why did the JAP smile on her wedding night?
Because she'd given her last blow job.

When do Jewish men stop masturbating?
When their wives die.

Why did the Polack feed nylon to his chickens?
He wanted them to lay L'eggs.

Why don't WASPs like sex?
Because you start at the top and work your way to the bottom.

What's a WASP's idea of a hand job?
A girl who'll suck on his fingers.

How can you tell a WASP widow is in mourning?
There's a black olive in her martini.

Why did the Mafia have Einstein killed?
Because he knew too much.

What did it say on the redneck's bumper sticker?
"I know Jack Shit."

How does the best-selling birthday card in Appalachia read?
"Happy Birthday, Uncle Daddy!"

Why don't Mexican dogs do tricks?
You have to be smarter than the dog to teach it tricks.

How do rednecks celebrate Halloween?
Pump kin.

How do you scare off a black mugger?
Threaten to wipe a booger on his new sneakers.

Why do Scotsmen wear kilts?
Sheep can hear a zipper a mile away.

How do Italian girls shave their legs?
They lay down and let someone mow them.

What's a bisexual hillbilly?
He screws his daughters and granddaughters.

What's a Puerto Rican's idea of safe sex?
Locking the car doors.

Why did the rich Polack love to beat off?
He was proud of being a self-made millionaire.

What do you call a skeleton in the closet?
Last year's Polish hide-and-seek winner.

What do you call a basement full of JAPs?
A whine cellar.

How do you know you're a redneck?
Your wife has a spit cup on the ironing board.

How do you know you're a redneck?
Your wife has come out of the bathroom and said, "Ya'll come look at this 'fore I flush it."

How do you know you're a redneck?
Your house has wheels and you car doesn't.

How do you know you're a redneck?
Directions to your house say "Turn off the paved road."

How do you know you're a redneck?
Your wife weighs more than your pick-up truck.

How do you know you're a redneck?
You think a Volvo is part of a woman's anatomy.

How do you know you're a redneck?
The most common phrase in your house is, "Someone go jiggle the handle."

How do you know you're a redneck?
You've been divorced and re-married three times and you still have the same in-laws.

How do you know you're a redneck?
Remodeling your bathroom means digging a new hole in the backyard.

How do you know you're a redneck?
You have more than one major appliance on your front porch.

How do you know you're a redneck?
You refer to the fifth grade as "my senior year."

How do you know you're a redneck?
You've taken a beer to a job interview.

How do you know you're a redneck?
Your senior prom had a day care center.

How do you know you're a redneck?
Your two-year-old has more teeth than you do.

How do you know you're a redneck?
You've eaten road-kill.

How do you know you're a redneck?
You keep a can of Crisco in the bedroom.

How do you know you're a redneck?
You stand under the mistletoe waiting for Granny or Cousin Sue Ellen to walk by.

How do you know you're a redneck?
Your idea of foreplay is slipping off her saddle.

How do you know you're a redneck?
You can't marry your sweetheart because there are laws against it.

How do you know you're a redneck?
The ASPCA raids your kitchen.

How do you know you're a redneck?
Your wife's hairdo was once ruined by a ceiling fan.

THE BEST GROSS BLONDE JOKES

How do blonde brain cells die?
Alone.

How do you brainwash a blonde?
Give her a douche and shake her upside down.

How do you change a blonde's mind?
Blow in her ear.

How do you measure a blonde's intelligence?
Stick a tire pressure gauge in her ear.

How do you get a blonde pregnant?
Come in her shoes and let the flies do the rest.

How do you get a blonde to marry you?
Tell her she's pregnant.
What will she ask you?
"Is it mine?"

How do you amuse a blonde for hours?
Write "Please turn over" on both sides of a piece of paper.

How does a blonde hold her liquor?
By the ears.

How does a blonde moonwalk?
She pulls down her panties and slides her ass along the floor.

Why are only two percent of blondes touch-typists?
The rest are hunt'n peckers.

What do you call a blond mother-in-law?
An air bag.

Why should you never take a blonde out for coffee?
It's too hard to re-train them.

What do blondes do for foreplay?
Remove their underwear.

———

What do blondes wear behind their ears to attract men?
Their heels.

———

What's the difference between a blonde and an ironing board?
It's difficult to open the legs of an ironing board.

———

What's the difference between a blonde and a broom closet?
Only two men fit inside a broom closet at once.

———

What's the difference between a blonde and a phone booth?
You need a quarter to use the phone.

———

What's the difference between a pit bull and a blonde with PMS?
Lipstick.

What do the Bermuda Triangle and blondes have in common?
They've both swallowed a lot of semen.

How does a blonde commit suicide?
She gathers her clothes into a pile and jumps off.

How do you plant dope?
Bury a blonde.

Why did God give blonds two percent more brains than horses?
Because he didn't want them shitting in the streets during parades.

How does the blond turn on the light after she has sex?
She opens the car door.

How does a blonde get pregnant?
And I thought blondes were dumb.

How does a blonde part her hair?
By doing the splits.

How do you get a blonde's eyes to twinkle?
Shine a torch in her ears.

How do you tell when a blonde reaches orgasm?
Who cares?

How do blondes pierce their ears?
They put tacks in their shoulder pads.

How does a blonde like her eggs?
Unfertilized.

How do you drown a blond?
Don't tell her to swallow.

How does a blonde high-five?
She smacks herself in the forehead.

How do you describe a blonde, surrounded by drooling idiots?
Flattered.

What do you call a blonde with ESP and PMS?
A know-it-all bitch.

What's the difference between a counterfeit dollar and a skinny blonde?
One's a phony buck and one's a bony fuck.

What's the difference between a chorus line of blondes and a magician?
A magician has a cunning array of stunts.

What does best blonde secretary in the world do?
She never misses a period.

What does a blonde think an innuendo is?
An Italian suppository.

What two airborne things can get a blonde pregnant?
Her feet.

How can you tell when a blonde is wearing pantyhose?
When she farts, her knees bag.

What's the disease that paralyzes blondes below the waist?
Marriage.

How do you describe the perfect blonde?
Three feet tall, no teeth, and a flat head to rest your beer on.

How do you confuse a blonde?
You don't. They're born that way.

How can you tell which blonde is the waitress?
She's the one with the tampon behind her ear, wondering what she did with her pencil.

How can you tell if a blonde's been using the computer?
There's white-out on the screen.

What's the difference between a blonde and a computer?
You only have to punch information into a computer once.

What did the blonde think of the new computer?
She didn't like it because she couldn't get channel nine.

How can you tell if a blonde has been in your refrigerator?
By the lipstick on your cucumbers.

How can you tell if a blonde works in an office?
A bed in the stockroom and huge smiles on all the bosses' faces.

How can you tell when a blonde is dating?
By the buckle print on her forehead.

Why do blondes write "T.G.I.F." inside their shoes?
To remind them: Toes Go In First!

What's the difference between a blonde and a guy?
The blonde has the higher sperm count.

What's the difference between a blonde and a trampoline?
You take off your shoes before using a trampoline.

What's the difference between Indiana and a blonde?
A blonde has larger hills and deeper valleys.

What's the difference between a blonde and a toothbrush?
You don't let your best friend borrow your toothbrush.

What is the difference between a blonde and a toilet?
A toilet won't follow you around after you use it.

What's the difference between a blonde and a rooster?
In the morning a rooster says, "Cocka-doodle-dooo," while a blonde says, "Any-cock'll-doooo."

What's the difference between a blonde and a limousine?
Not everybody has been in a limousine.

What's the difference between a blonde and a bowling ball?
They're both round and have three holes to poke.

What's the difference between a blonde and the Grand Old Duke of York?
The Grand Old Duke of York only "had" 10,000 men.

Why is it good to have a blonde passenger?
You can park in the handicap zone.

Why is a blonde like a turtle?
They both get fucked up when they're on their backs.

Why does NASA hire peroxide blondes?
They're doing research on black holes.

Why does a blonde insist that her lover wear a condom?
So she can have a doggie bag for later.

Why do men like blonde jokes?
Because they can understand them.

Why do blondes like lightning?
They think someone is taking their picture.

Why do blondes have a dimple on their chin and a flat forehead?
Finger on chin—I don't know. Hits forehead—Oh I get it!

Why do blondes have two more brain cells than a cow?
So that when you pull their tits, they don't moo.

Why do blondes drive BMWs?
Because they can spell it.

Why do blondes have big bellybuttons?
From dating blonde men.

Why do blondes put their hair in ponytails?
To cover up the valve stem.

Why do blondes have square boobs?
Because they forgot to take the tissues out of the box.

Why do blondes take the pill?
So they know what day of the week it is.

Why do blondes like tilt steering?
More head room.

Why do blondes drive cars with sunroofs?
More leg room.

Why do blondes wear underwear?
They make good ankle warmers.

Why do blondes wear green lipstick?
Because red means stop.

Why do blondes wear hoop earings?
They have to have someplace to rest their ankles.

Why don't blondes eat bananas?
They can't find the zipper.

Why don't blondes use vibrators?
They chip their teeth.

What is the worst thing about sex with a blonde?
Bucket seats.

What do you call a blonde touching her toes?
A brunette with bad breath.

If a blonde and a brunette are tossed off a building, who hits the ground first?
The brunette. The blonde has to stop to ask directions.

What happens when a blonde gets Alzheimer's disease?
Her IQ goes up.

Why is a washing machine better than a blonde?
Because you can drop your load in a washing machine and it won't follow you around for a week.

What do blondes and cow-pats have in common?
They both get easier to pick up with age.

What does a peroxide blonde and a 747 have in common?
They both have a black box and a cockpit.

What does a blonde say if you blow in her ear?
"Thanks for the refill."

What do blondes do after they comb their hair?
They pull up their pants.

What do you call a blonde lesbian?
A waste.

What do you call five blondes at the bottom of the pool?
Air bubbles.

What do you call four blondes lying on the ground?
An air mattress.

What do you call a blonde behind a steering wheel?
An air bag.

What do you call a blonde between two brunettes?
A mental block.

What do you call ten blondes standing ear to ear?
A wind tunnel.

What do you call fifteen blondes in a circle?
A dope ring.

———

What do you call a blonde with two brain cells?
Pregnant.

———

What do you call a blonde with a dollar on the top of her head?
All you can eat, under a buck.

———

What do you call a brunette with a blonde on either side?
An interpreter.

———

What do you call twenty blondes in a freezer?
Frosted Flakes.

———

What do you call a fly buzzing inside a blonde's head?
A Space Invader.

What do you call a smart blonde?
A golden retriever.

What do you see when you look into a blonde's eyes?
The back of her head.

What do you call it when a blonde dies her hair brunette?
Artificial intelligence.

What do blondes say after sex?
"Are all you guys all on the same team?"

What do a blonde and a beer bottle have in common?
They're both empty from the neck up.

What does a blonde owl say?
"What, what?"

How many blondes does it take to make chocolate chip cookies?
Three—one to mix the batter and two to squeeze the rabbit.

What's the blonde's cheer?
"I'm blonde, I'm blonde, I'm B-L-O-N . . . Oh well. I'm blonde, I'm blonde, yeah yeah yeah . . ."

Why did the blonde have a sore navel?
Because her boyfriend was also blond.

Why did the blonde want to become a veterinarian?
Because she loved children.

Why did they call the blond "Twinkie?"
She liked to be filled with cream.

What is the irritating part around a blonde's vagina?
The blonde.

What's black and fuzzy and hangs from the ceiling?
A blonde electrician.

How do we know that the Virgin Mary wasn't blonde?
You can't have a baby at age six.

Why are blondes like cornflakes?
Because they're simple, easy and they taste good.

Why are there no dumb brunettes?
Peroxide.

What did the blonde's right leg say to the left leg?
Nothing—they've never met.

What's the mating call of the blonde?
"I'm *sooo* drunk."

What is the mating call of the ugly blonde?
(Screaming) "I said, I'm drunk!"

What's a blonde's favorite nursery rhyme?
Hump-me Dump-me.

Why are there lipstick stains on the steering wheel after a blonde drives a car?
'Cause she blows the horn.

What is the difference between a blonde and a refrigerator?
A refrigerator doesn't fart when you pull your meat out of it.

How would a blond punctuate the following? "Fun fun fun worry worry worry"
Fun period fun period fun NO PERIOD worry worry worry.

What are love handles to a blonde?
Her ears.

THE BEST GROSS CELEBRITY JOKES

What do you call Newt Gingrich and Bob Dole sitting in the front seat of your car?
Dual airbags.

If Newt Gingrich, Bob Dole, and Pat Buchanan jumped off the world Trade Center, who would hit first?
Who cares!

Why did Newt Gingrich's proctologist call?
He finally found Newt's head.

What is the difference between Newt Gingrich and the Hindenburg?
One is a big fat Nazi gas bag and the other was an aircraft.

Newt Gingrich, Bob Dole, and Pat Buchanan are all alone on a deserted island. Who survives?
We do!

———

What's the difference between Newt Gingrich and a catfish?
One's a scum-sucking-bottom-dweller and one's a fish.

———

How can you tell the weather's really hot?
Madonna's sleeping with only two people on top of her.

———

What are Newt Gingrich's chances of becoming president?
Excellent—if the Democrats nominate Saddam Hussein.

———

Why did Yassir Arrafat visit 42nd Street when he was visiting the United Nations?
He was practicing his piece negotiations.

What's the difference between the sex life of the average man and the sex life of the average Congressman?
The average man has had seven sex partners since the age of 18; the average Congressman has had seven sex partners under the age of 18.

———

What would happen if you merged Domino's Pizza with the U.S. Postal Service?
Your pizza would arrive in thirty days.

———

Have you tried the new Ben & Jerry's ice cream flavor?
Bury Garcia.

———

Did you hear what Jerry Garcia died from?
Acid indigestion.

———

What did one Deadhead say to the other Deadhead when his drugs wore off?
"Boy, they were right—this music really does suck!"

How do you know when Deadheads break into your house?
They're still living there three months later.

———

How many Deadheads does it takes to screw in a lightbulb?
None. They wait till it burns out, then they follow it around the country.

———

What did Jerry Garcia say to Elvis Presley when he got to heaven?
"You'll never guess who your daughter married."

———

Why is *The Rush Limbaugh Show* like *Barney?*
Both feature a bunch of intellectually underdeveloped fans fawning over a big fat shallow puppet.

———

How many Rush Limbaughs does it take to screw in a lightbulb?
Only one. He holds the lightbulb and the world revolves around him.

What's the difference between Rush Limbaugh and a whale?
A sportscoat.

———

If you were in a room with Hitler, Mussolini and Rush Limbaugh and you only had two bullets, what should you do?
Shoot Rush twice!

———

What happens when Rush Limbaugh visits McDonalds?
They add another "0" to the sign.

———

What's longer than a city block and has a brain the size of a peanut?
The ticket line at *The Rush Limbaugh Show.*

———

A dog and Rush Limbaugh have been run over by a semi on a deserted California highway. What is the difference?
There are skid marks in front of the dog.

On which vehicle are you most likely to see a "Rush is Right" bumper sticker?
The one blowing the most smoke.

———

What's the difference between Roseanne and poultry?
Most poultry is dressed better.

———

Did you hear they renamed Hugh Grant's movie, *Nine Months?*
It's now called, *Nine Months to a Year.*

———

Why did Hugh Grant trade in his car?
He wanted one with more head room.

———

What's the difference between Hugh Grant and a camel?
A camel doesn't have to pay for humps.

———

Do you know the difference between a white BMW and a hotel room?
No? Neither does Hugh Grant!

What is Hugh Grant's favorite breakfast cereal?
Trix.

———

How do we know Hugh Grant is modest?
He doesn't blow his own horn.

———

What do Hugh Grant and Faye Dunaway have in common?
Both got screwed on Sunset Boulevard.

———

Why is Congress so tough on criminals?
When it comes to stealing, they don't like competition.

———

If the band plays "Hail To The Chief" when the President enters a room, what does it play when Newt Gingrich comes in?
"Send In The Clowns."

———

What's the only thing less exciting than hearing Al Gore speak?
Watching Roseanne get undressed.

Why is Dennis Rodman like Joseph of Nazareth?
They both fucked a Madonna.

———

Who was Tinkerbell's abortionist?
Captain Hook.

———

How did Captain Hook die?
He wiped with the wrong hand.

———

Why is the FBI suspicious of Washington D.C. Mayor Marion Barry?
They found him trying to snort the White House.

———

How do you say Magic Johnson's name in Chinese?
Coon-Die-Soon.

———

What do Winnie-the-Pooh and John-the-Baptist have in common?
Same middle name.

What was O.J.'s favorite play in the Buffalo Bills' playbook?
Cut left, slash right.

Why did O.J. kill his ex?
He wanted to terminate her free agency.

Who's the most famous Los Angeles Dodger?
O.J. Simpson.

What's the difference between O.J. Simpson and John Elway?
One drives a slow, white Bronco. The other is a slow, white Bronco.

What's OJ's favorite baseball team (besides the Dodgers)?
The Red Sox!

Did you hear about Hertz's new billboard?
It's a picture of O.J. Simpson with the caption, "Hertz: For Great Getaways!"

What were Nicole Simpson's last words?
"Stop, O.J.! It Hertz!"

Did you hear about the new O.J. Simpson movie?
It's called, *Sex, Knives, and Athletic Tape.*

How do you get an electric chair to work?
Give it the Juice!

What did the LAPD and Tropicana have in common?
They both had O.J. in a can.

What is the difference between Tang and O.J.?
Tang won't kill you!

Why do they call him O.J.?
Because he beats the pulp out of his women.

Did you hear about the new drink called the Bloody Nicole?
It's like a Bloody Mary, but instead of tomato juice, you add O.J.!

What was the last thing Nicole Simpson said?
"I should have had a V-8."

What did O.J. do when he saw the cops in his rearview mirror?
He froze and concentrated.

What's black and white and red all over?
O.J. paying a visit to his ex-wife.

Why does everyone want O.J. over for Thanksgiving dinner?
He knows how to slice the hell out of white meat.

Why did O.J. stop at his ex-wife's house on his way to the airport?
He had some time to kill.

What role did a marriage counselor play in Nicole's murder?
When O.J. wanted a reconciliation, the counselor told him to take a stab at it.

What did O.J. say to Goldman when he found him with his ex-wife?
"Hey pal, mind if I cut in?"

What is O.J.'s favorite soft drink?
Orange Slice.

What is O.J.'s motto?
"If you can't beat 'em, stab 'em."

What do O.J. Simpson and Michael Jackson have in common?
They are both missing a glove.

What did Michael Jackson say to O.J. Simpson?
"Don't worry, I'll take care of the kids."

Did you hear John Wayne Bobbit called O.J.?
He wanted to tell O.J. that he knows what it feels like to be separated from a loved one.

What's the difference between Jeffrey Dahmer and O.J. Simpson?
O.J. only ate one of his victims.

Did you hear that Joey Buttafuocco went to visit O.J. in prison?
He told O.J. that he should have had his girlfriend do it.

What would you have if O.J. was put in a cell with David Koresh and Jeffrey Dahmer?
A complete breakfast: serial, toast, and O.J.

What's the only thing worse than being married to Lorena Bobbitt?
Being divorced from O.J. Simpson.

What's the difference between O.J. and Christopher Reeve?
Reeve has feelings from the neck up.

What do O.J. and Christopher Reeve have in common?
Both left blood on the Bronco.

Why can't Heidi Fleiss and O.J. Simpson play golf together?
Because Heidi Fleiss is a hooker and O.J. Simpson is a slicer.

What's the last thing O.J. said to Nicole Simpson?
"Your waiter will be with you shortly."

What are two things that O.J. has that every man wants?
A Heisman Trophy and a dead wife.

What do O.J. and Tampax have in common?
They both come in white boxes and leave a bloody mess.

Why didn't Nicole Simpson go out drinking with her friends after dinner?
She wanted to go home and get ripped.

Why didn't Nicole's other boyfriends go down on her?
Because they knew the Juice would kill them.

What was the murder weapon in the Nicole Brown case?
A six-foot spade.

Did you hear O.J. is getting married again?
I hope he doesn't cut the bride and kiss the cake.

What's the difference between J.F.K. and Nicole Simpson?
We're not 100 percent sure who killed J.F.K.

How many O.J. jurors does it take to screw in a lightbulb?
None. They voted that it was "not dark."

What do Mark Fuhrman and O.J. have in common?
Neither one of them likes to hang out with black folks.

What was O.J.'s first meal after being released?
Chicken, white and well-battered.

What do Marcia Clark and Susan Smith have in common?
Neither one got the Juice.

Did you hear that Ronald Reagan called O.J. to congratulate him on the verdict?
Afterwards, he invited O.J. and Nicole over for dinner.

What is the NRA's new motto?
Guns don't kill people, O.J. does.

What is the world's worst golf foursome?
O.J. Simpson, Heidi Fleiss, Susan Smith, and Greg Louganis. O.J. is always slicing, Heidi is always hooking, Susan is always in the water, and Greg is always in the wrong hole.

Did you hear about the new O.J. ride at Disneyland?
It's a dollar to get on, but $5 million to get off.

What's the difference between Mark Fuhrman and a black woman?
A black woman can't get O.J. off.

THE BEST GROSS RELIGIOUS JOKES

An old priest and a nun were traveling to a remote desert mission when their camel got sick and fell to the ground, dead. They walked for hours, but encountered only endless sand. Certain their fate was hopeless, the priest was overcome by a fierce desire to experience sex once before he died. He pulled out his dick, then turned to the nun and asked, "Sister, do you know what this is?"

"No," she replied.

The priest said, "It's the staff of life."

"Great," the nun exclaimed. "Then stick it up that camel's ass and let's ride out of here!"

How do we know the Virgin Mary was a bitch?
Because the Bible says she rode Joseph's ass all the way to Bethlehem.

What do you get when you cross a Jehovah's Witness and an agnostic?
Someone who knocks on your door for no particular reason.

What do nuns and 7-Up have in common?
"Never had it, never will."

———

What happened to the nun who got tired of using candles?
She called in an electrician.

———

What's black and white and black and white and black and white and black and white and black and white and black and white and black and white?
A nun falling down the stairs.

———

What's the newest rage among nuns?
A vibrating crucifix.

———

What did the Bishop do when Father Maguire confessed that he was so horny he was constantly aroused?
Got down on his knees, prayed, then licked the problem.

———

Why do priests have no problem believing in the Holy Spirit?
Most of them are fairies.

Why are so many priests alcoholics?
They're drawn to the pure in spirit.

What's black and white and has a hole in the middle?
A nun.

When a priest makes the sign of the cross, what is he thankful for?
That they crucified Christ instead of castrating him.

Why wasn't Christ born in Italy?
They couldn't find three wise men and a virgin.

Why are there so few Polish monks?
The vow of silence includes farting.

Why did the Pope flash the Sistine Chapel?
He wanted to expose himself to art.

Early one morning in rural Ireland two leprechauns knocked on the door of a convent and asked for the Mother Superior.

The Mother Superior comes out and the older of the two leprechauns asks, "Mother Superior, are there any wee little leprechaun nuns in this convent?"

Rather startled and bemused the Mother Superior says, "No, there aren't any wee little leprechaun nuns in this convent."

"Well then," asks the older leprechaun, "are there any wee little leprechaun nuns at any convent in this county?"

Even more confused than bemused the Mother Superior says, "No, there aren't any wee little leprechaun nuns in any convent in this county."

"Well let me ask you one more question then," says the older leprechaun, "Do you know of any wee little leprechaun nuns at any convent in any county in all of Ireland?"

Now confused and a little bewildered Mother Superior says, "No, I know of no wee little leprechaun nuns at any convent in any county in all of Ireland."

The younger of the two leprechauns is now looking very downcast, staring at his shoes. Then the older leprechaun puts his hands on his hips and turns to the younger one and says, "There you go Sean, you heard her, I told you you were fucking a penguin!"

There were three nuns sitting on a park bench. A man walks up and flashes them. The first nun has a stroke, the second nun has a stroke, the third nun couldn't reach!

How do you get a nun pregnant?
Dress her up like an altar boy.

How about the two nuns returning to the convent from doing some shopping on their push bikes?
One says, "I've never come this way before." The other one says, "It must be the cobblestones."

Four nuns go out for a weekend. On Monday they come back and need to confess their sins.

The first nun goes into the confessional and says, "Father I have sinned. I touched a penis with this finger."

The father says, "You are forgiven, just swirl your hand in the holy water."

The second goes in. "Father I have sinned. I fondled a package with this hand."

The father says, "You are forgiven, just clean off your hand in the holy water."

The third nun is about to go in when the fourth says, "Sister, may I please go ahead of you? Otherwise I'll be drinking what you sit in."

Three altar boys are standing in the snow with their pants down around their ankles and their penises in a snow bank. Sister Margaret sticks her head out the window and says, "Boys! Boys! Whatever are you doing? You're going to catch pneumonia. Put your penises away!"

The tallest altar boy turns around and yells, "Sister Margaret, don't worry, we know what we're doing. Father Porter always likes a couple cold ones after work!"

Did you hear about the new religious group called Jehovah's Bystanders?
They're Witnesses who don't want to get involved.

How do we know God is not a woman?
In four billion years, the stars have never been rearranged.

What is the priest's favorite soup?
Cream of Altar Boy.

How do you spell priest in Latin?
P-e-d-o-p-h-i-l-e.

What's another phrase for a nun's pussy?
A Bible pelt.

What's a priest's idea of celibacy?
Only two altar boys a week.

What did the inscriptions "INRI" on Christ's cross stand for?
"I'm nailed right in."

Why is an altar boy like a Catholic church?
Both are frequently entered from the rear.

Why does an altar boy usually get good grades?
Behind every altar boy is a priest, pushing.

THE BEST ALL-AROUND GROSS JOKES

How come Helen Keller can't have kids?
Because she's DEAD!

How did Helen Keller drive herself crazy?
Trying to read a stucco wall.

What is Helen Keller's favorite color?
Corduroy.

How did Helen Keller burn the side of her face?
She answered the iron.

How did she burn the other side of her face?
They called back.

How did Helen Keller's parents punish her?
They left the plunger in.

Why was Helen Keller's leg wet?
Her dog was blind, too.

Why did Helen Keller masturbate with one hand?
She needed the other to moan with.

What did Helen Keller do when she fell down the well?
Screamed her fingers off.

How come Helen Keller didn't scream when she fell off the cliff?
She was wearing mittens.

Why does Helen Keller wear skin-tight pants?
So you can read her lips

Why did Helen Keller's dog commit suicide?
You would too if your name was "Urghrrghrghr."

Have you heard of the new Helen Keller doll?
Wind it up and it walks into walls.

What's this (slowly waving fingers)?
Helen Keller moaning.

Who is the cruelest man in the world?
The guy who raped Helen Keller, then cut off her hands so she couldn't scream for help.

What happened after the cannibal ate a priest, a rabbi, and a Muslim cleric?
He had an ecumenical movement.

Why did the vampire only drive on I-95?
It was the main artery.

How would you describe the average cannibal?
A guy who had a wife and ate children.

What did the cannibal say when he saw a skating rink?
"What do you know, people on the rocks!"

Did you hear about the cannibal who went to an "all you can eat" restaurant?
He had two waiters and a bus boy.

Did you hear about the cannibal nymphomaniac?
Every time her tribe ate a missionary, she insisted on the bone.

What happens if you visit a cannibal religious ceremony?
You'll be thoroughly stirred.

Why did the cannibal put a Mexican in the blender?
He wanted bean soup.

———

Why don't cannibals eat Jewish children?
They're always spoiled.

———

How can you tell a gay cannibal?
He always blows lunch.

———

What's a cannibal bachelor party?
A girl jumps out of a cake, then everyone has a piece.

———

What did the leper say to the prostitute?
Keep the tip!

———

Why did they call off the leper poker tourney?
Somebody threw in their hand.

Why did they call off the leper hockey game?
There was a face off in the corner.

———

Did you hear about the leper that was a big hit at the party?
They were using his back for clam dip.

———

Why is sex with a leper the best?
Because you always get a souvenir.

———

What do you call five lepers in a hot tub?
Soup.

———

Why did the leper fail his driving test?
He left his foot on the accelerator.

———

What do you call a leper in a bath?
Porridge.

Why did the leper gigolo have to quit his job?
His business kept falling off.

———

How do you make leper sausage?
Hang a sock in a wind tunnel and throw a leper in.

———

How do you make spaghetti with a leper?
Hit him in the head with a tennis racket.

———

How can you tell when you get a letter from a leper?
The tongue is in the envelope.

———

Did you hear about the new chain of African restaurants?
You walk in and they eat you.

———

Did you hear about the new resort for people who limp?
It's called Club Foot.

THE BEST GROSS HOMOSEXUAL JOKES

What do they call the barracks for gay soldiers?
Head quarters.

How do fags fuck?
Bend over and find out.

How do you get AIDS from a toilet seat?
By sitting down before the last guy who used it stands up.

What's the difference between a sodomist and a suppository?
None.

What do you call an open can of tuna fish sitting in a dresser drawer?
Lesbian potpourri.

Why were gays the first to clear out of San Francisco after the earthquake?
They already had their shit packed.

What's the AIDS hotline number?
1-800-TOO-LATE.

———

Why are hairdressers such pricks?
You are what you eat.

———

What do a gay prostitute and a lawyer have in common?
They both make a living fucking people up the ass.

———

Why are gays the least lonely people?
They have friends up the ass.

———

Why did the gay detective get fired?
He blew all his cases.

———

What does it mean when two lesbians make love?
It doesn't mean dick.

What do you call a faggot who's into S&M?
A sucker for punishment.

———

What are the most popular merit badges for gay Cub Scouts?
First AIDS, Foreskin Diving, and Semenship.

———

"Daddy, Daddy, what's a transvestite?"
"Shut up and unhook my bra."

———

Why are homosexual novels so predictable?
The hero always gets his man in the end.

———

Did you hear about the new AIDS hospital outside of Atlanta?
It's called Sick Fags Over Georgia.

———

What do you get when you cross a homosexual and an insect?
An asshopper.

Why are fags like killer bees?
Their leader is a queen and their pricks are fatal.

———

Did you hear about the new lesbian-run Baskin-Robbins?
The flavor of the month is anchovy.

———

Did you hear about the new lesbian-run Baskin-Robbins?
The ice cream cones have hair on them.

———

How can you tell you're in a lesbian-run Baskin-Robbins?
They hand you the cone upside down.

What's the cone made of?
Dil-dough.

———

Did you hear they finally jailed all the transvestite hookers?
They charged them with violating the Truth-in-Lending Act.

Why are fags so polite?
They'll give their seat to anyone.

What's a bisexual gentleman?
A guy who takes out a girl three times before he fucks her brother.

What does a housewife do when she's depressed?
Goes to the mall to try on a few new things.
What does a fag do when he's depressed?
Goes to a gay bar and tries a few new things.

What does a fag call a wad of cum in a baggie?
Fast food.

Did you hear about the new book about how AIDS spreads?
It's called *Grim Fairy Tales.*

How did the hairdresser get a bad case of diarrhea?
All he ate were fruits.

How can you tell you're in Greenwich Village?
The crosswalk signs flash, "Kneel . . . Don't Kneel."

What's a lesbian's favorite pet?
A lap dog.

What do you call an African-American fag?
A brotherfucker.

What do Good Humor trucks sell in San Francisco?
Spermsicles.

Why do gay golfers love Mexico?
Every day they have a hole in Juan.

How can you tell if two truckers are gay?
They exchange loads.

Why did the fag beat off into the strawberry preserves?
He wanted a penis butter and jelly sandwich.

What's the new lesbian bumper sticker?
"Save a tree. Eat a beaver."

———

Why is a frog like a faggot?
The minute they see a fly, their tongues come out.

———

Why go gays love movie ushers?
They can always find a seat in the dark.

———

Why don't blondes in San Francisco wear short black mini skirts?
'Cause their balls show.

THE BEST GROSS ANIMAL JOKES

What do you call a rabbit with a bent dick?
Fucks Funny!

Did you hear about the guy that entered his dog at the pet show?
He got sixteen months.

What's the largest drawback in the jungle?
An elephant's foreskin.

What do a walrus and a Tupperware box have in common?
They both like a tight seal.

A farmer and his wife were lying in bed one evening; she was knitting, he was reading the latest issue of *Animal Husbandry.* He looks up from the page and says to her, "Did you know that humans are the only species in which the female achieves orgasm?"

She looks at him and replies, "Oh, yeah? Prove it."

He frowns for moment, but says, "O.K." He then gets up and walks out, leaving his wife with a confused look on her face.

About a half hour later he returns, tired and sweaty, and proclaims, "Well I'm sure the cow and sheep didn't, but the way that pig's always squealing, how can I tell?"

———

What do you call a deer with no eyes?
No idea.

What do you call a deer with no eyes and no legs?
Still no idea.

What do you call a deer with no eyes and no legs, chewing on a razor blade?
Still no bloody idea.

What do you call a deer with no feet, legs, torso, neck, or head?
A hat rack.

What do you call a deer with no eyes, no legs, and no balls?
Still no fucking eye deer.

What did the mother gerbil say to her babies?
"Now, don't you go hanging around any assholes!"

———

What's so different about a Siberian tiger?
It's a pussy that eats you.

———

Why do squirrels swim upside down?
To keep their nuts dry.

———

Did you hear about the thin guy who went to Alaska?
He came back a husky fucker.

———

What has four legs and one arm?
A pit bull.

———

How do pigs have babies?
They pork each other.

What do you call an Australian with a sheep under each arm?
A baa-sexual.

Why are elephants who use sheep for tampons so fat?
Sheep don't come with strings.

What's a mutton button?
A sheep's clitoris.

How can you tell a guy's a real pervert?
He sees an elephant and exclaims, "Wow! 436-224-436!"

Did you hear about the gay whale?
He'd bite off the end of a submarine and swallow the seamen.

Why did the female robin build a nest with a hole in the middle?
She loved laying eggs but hated kids.

Did you hear about the farmer that was into S&M?
He chained up the sheep before he fucked them.

Did you hear about the farmer who fell in love with his cow?
It was udder madness.

What do you give an elephant with diarrhea?
Lots of room.

Why do frogs have the worst sex life?
They hop on, hop off, then they croak.

How do you know your girlfriend has bad gas?
You find a skunk proposing to one of her farts.

Why did the Australian go to the pet cemetery?
To visit his childhood sweetheart.

Why do elephants have long toenails?
To pick their trunks.

What did the little boy say when he saw the rabbit humping the cat?
"Look, hare on a pussy!"

What do you get from fucking cows?
Steeroids.

———

What's was Moby Dick's father's name?
Papa Boner.

———

What do you get when you cross a groundhog and a vibrator?
An armadildo.

———

What do you get when you cross a steer and a Polack?
Bullshit.

———

What do you get when you cross a cobra with a pair of corduroys?
A trouser snake.

———

What do you get when you trade your wife for a skunk?
A better-smelling pussy.

THE BEST GROSS SENIOR CITIZEN JOKES

What's the advantage of fucking old women?
They don't yell, they don't tell, they don't swell, and they're grateful as hell.

———

"Hey, Grandpa," little Timmy called, "can you make a noise like a frog?"

"Why do you want to know?" Grandpa said fondly.

"Because," the little boy said, "Mommy said that when you croak, we're all going to Disneyworld."

———

What's the best thing about having Alzheimer's Disease?
You meet new people every day.

What's the second best thing about having Alzheimer's Disease?
You can hide your own Easter eggs.

What's a wild night in the nursing home?
Giving every resident a full bottle of Ex-Lax so they'll have something to do.

What do old women have between their tits that young women don't?
A belly button.

What's a sure sign you're getting old?
You have to use tenderizer on your oatmeal.

What's a sure sign you're getting old?
You're playing post office, and they send you to the dead letter office.

What's a sure sign you're getting old?
You're favorite four letter word in bed is "H-E-L-P."

One guy said to a friend, "You know, I finally realized I'm getting older."

"How?"

"My wife gave up sex for Lent."

"So what?"

"So, I didn't realize it until the Fourth of July."

How do you know an old maid is aging?
She switches from cucumbers to butternut squash.

Did you hear about the new "no frills" nursing homes? Instead of providing three meals a day, they leave out large bowls of Ken-L-Ration.

How can you tell you're getting old?
When you find yourself saying, "You mean, it comes in both ointment *and* suppository?"

How can you tell you're really old?
You remember when AYDS was a diet candy.

Why is an old man like cement?
It takes both two days to get hard.

How can you tell your wife is getting old?
Her tit size is 34-long.

How can you tell your wife is getting old?
Her tits give powdered milk.

Did you hear about the new erotic clothing for old people?
Crotchless Depends.

How do you make an old maid's birthday cake?
Stick lit candles in the batter and the cake bakes itself.

How do you know you're getting old?
The only time you breath heavily at night is when you walk up the stairs.

What's the definition of embarrassment?
Two thirty-nine-year-old women meeting in the Social Security Office.

Why did the old maid buy two candles?
In case she wanted to light one.

Why is it cruel to make old people give up smoking?
Coughing and wheezing is the only exercise they get.

How did the old woman know she'd had too many face-lifts?
When she raised her eyebrows, her stockings tore.

How do you know you're getting old?
When you tell your buddy you spent the day with a hooker, he knows you've been playing golf.

What's middle age?
When you move from hardball to softball.

Why don't old women wear belts?
They can't tighten them because their tits get in the way.

THE BEST GROSS SEX JOKES

What do women and spaghetti have in common?
They both squirm when you eat them.

What did the hurricane say to the coconut tree?
Hold on to your nuts, this is no ordinary blow job.

Why was Snow White kicked out of Disneyland?
They found her sitting on Pinnochio's nose.

Fred was in jail for five long years, but his girlfriend Jill remained faithful to him. On his first night home, she took his hand and said, "Fred, I know this might be difficult for you after all this time, so if there's anything special you'd like me to do—go fast, go slow, anything—just say it and I'll do it."

"Well," he said, "there are two things."

"Name them."

"First," he said, "I'd like to take you from behind, doggy style, up the ass."

She grimaced, but said, "Okay. And what's the second thing?"

He replied, "Can I call you Bruce?"

What do you do in case of fallout?
Put it back in and take shorter strokes.

Why do women have two holes so close together?
In case you miss.

How do you tell if a woman is wearing underwear?
Look for dandruff on her shoes.

What's the ultimate in rejection?
When your right hand falls asleep.

What is organic dental floss?
Pubic hair.

What do you call grit in a condom?
An organ grinder.

What did the banana say to the vibrator?
"What are you shaking for? I'm the one she's going to EAT!"

Why is a pool table green?
Well, if someone racked your balls, you'd be green too.

Why did the condom fly across the room?
Because it got pissed off.

Did you hear about the flasher who was thinking of retiring?
He decided to stick it out for one more year.

What do you call a whore with her own car?
Feels on Wheels.

A man walks into a jewelers, unzips his trousers, and places his tool upon the counter. The lady serving him says, "I'm sorry sir, this is a clock shop, not a cock shop."

"Well, put two hands on this," replies the man.

Which of the following doesn't belong?
(a) meat
(b) eggs
(c) wife
(d) blowjob.
Answer: (d) a blowjob, because it's possible to beat your meat, your eggs, or your wife, but you can't beat a blowjob.

What's 69 and 69?
Dinner for four.

What's worse than lobsters on your piano?
Crabs on your organ.

How do you make a hormone?
Don't pay her.

What's the difference between 'ohh' and 'ahh'?
About four inches.

When does a Cub become a Boy Scout?
When he eats his first Brownie.

What's the difference between like and love?
Spit and swallow.

What's the difference between men and jelly beans?
Jelly beans come in different colors.

What do a Rubik's cube and a penis have in common?
The longer you play with it, the harder it gets!

Why do female paratroopers wear jockstraps?
So they don't whistle on the way down.

What do a coffin and a condom have in common?
They're both filled with stiffs—only one's coming and one's going.

Why did the nymphomaniac take her vibrator to the beach?
So she could shake and bake.

What does a pregnant woman and a burnt cake have in common?
You should have taken it out sooner.

Did you hear about the new all-women package delivery service?
It's called UPMS—they deliver whenever the fuck they feel like it.

Why did the hooker give up giving blow jobs and become a computer programmer?
Less down time.

What's a housewife?
An attachment you screw on the bed to get the housework done.

Why don't women have brains?
They don't have a dick to put them in.

Why do bald men cut holes in their pockets?
So they can let their fingers run through their hair.

Did you hear about the hermaphrodite baby?
It was born with a penis AND a brain.

What did the penis say to the condom?
"Cover me! I'm going in."

How many male chauvinists does it take to change a lightbulb?
None. Let the bitch do it herself after she's finished with the dishes.

Why is a penis like a balloon?
The more you blow, the bigger it gets.

What's the best way to keep a hard-on?
Don't fuck with it.

What's the difference between a paycheck and a penis?
You can always find a girl to blow your paycheck.

What do you call a man with a torn condom?
Daddy.

What's another word for tit-fucking?
Peak performance.

What's the difference between driving in fog and engaging in 69?
At least in 69, you can see the asshole in front of you.

What are the three words you don't want to hear while you're making love?
"Honey, I'm home!"

What's the difference between sex for money and sex for free?
Sex for free costs a lot more.

Did you hear about the new college course called "Intercourse 101?"
You take it between periods and all you have to do is come.

Why is 88 better than 69?
You get "ate" twice.

How do you know you're really lonely?
Your own tongue feels good in your mouth.

What's a doggie bra?
It makes pointers out of setters.

Why do nudists have the best parties?
On the dance floor, things are really swinging.

How did the hooker know the cop meant business?
When he showed her his nightstick.

Did you hear about the massage parlor girl who rubbed her customers the wrong way?
Instead of coming, they went.

How can you tell your date's really ugly?
When you take her to dinner, the waiter puts her plate on the floor.

How can you tell a guy's a loser?
He hires a hooker and she tells him, "Not on the first date."

What's a faithful Hollywood husband?
One whose alimony checks arrive on time.

Why is a hooker like a Xerox salesman?
They both lease reproduction equipment.

How can you tell a woman is really flat?
She interviews for a job as a topless waitress and gets hired as a bus boy.

How can you tell a guy is a loser?
His only sex life is when the doctor says, "Cough."

Why are impotent men immature?
They were born, but never raised.

Why is a hooker like a cattle rancher?
They both raise meat.

Did you know that hookers use poor grammar?
They end every sentence with a proposition.

Why did they call the coed "Turnpike?"
Once you got on, you never had to stop.

Why did the whore get fired by the madam?
She was discovered standing up on the job.

Did you hear about the Wall Street firm that merged with an S&M whorehouse?
They now offer stocks and bondage.

What happened to the girl who swallowed a razor blade?
In a week, she gave herself a hysterectomy, castrated her husband, circumcised her lover, took two fingers off her girlfriend's hand, and gave her minister a harelip.

Why is it painful to fuck a chef?
He sticks a fork in you to find out if you're done.

How do you know your date's a loser?
His favorite sex aid is Fix-A-Flat.

What's the best way to stop a guy from smoking after sex?
Fill his waterbed with gasoline.

Why are anchovies like telephones?
They're the next best thing to being there.

What's the golf tournament for flashers?
The Zipper Open.

Why do carpenters make lousy lovers?
They're used to putting their tools in the box after they're done.

How do you know your date's a loser?
All his soap has holes drilled in it.

How do you know your date's a loser?
His teddy bear has an artificial vagina.

How do you know if you have a small penis?
Your date asks if she can use it to get out a splinter.

How do you know who you're going to fuck today?
Look it up in your whore-o-scope.

Why is Kotex such a potent international weapon?
It keeps the Reds in, the Poles out, the Greeks happy, and the French hungry.

What do you call it when a hooker comes to your hotel room?
Womb service.

How do you celebrate a vasectomy?
With a bottle of Dry Sac.

How do you know your date's ugly?
A mosquito bites her, then throws up.

Why is it hard to pronounce "fellatio?"
It's a mouthful.

Why is a penis like payday?
It can't come too often.

Why was the loser so frustrated?
He finally woke up with an erection and discovered both hands were asleep.

How can you tell a woman is really ugly?
She even turns off her vibrator.

How can you tell if your date is really flat?
She has "front" tattooed on her chest.

How can you tell your date is really flat?
When you look down her dress, all you see is her corns.

What's the definition of ugly?
Your date looks like she ran out of money halfway through a sex change operation.

The guy climbed on top. A minute later he complained, "Hey, you don't have any tits and your cunt's way too tight."

The woman yelled, "Get off my back!"

Why is a loser like a microwave?
He heats up instantly, then goes "ding" in thirty seconds.

Why is a loser like a rodeo rider?
They both stay on for eight seconds.

What's it like to make love to a loser?
Ever try stuffing a marshmallow into a parking meter slot?

How do you describe a loser's sex life?
Fist or famine.

How do you know you've got a really small dick?
When your girlfriend takes it in her mouth, she doesn't suck, she flosses.

What happened when the loser called the telephone sex line?
The girl said, "Not tonight, I've got an earache."

Why are men so good at reading maps?
Only a man could conceive that one inch equals 100 miles.

How can you tell your girlfriend is really fat?
The back of her neck looks like a pack of hot dogs.

How can you tell your girlfriend is really fat?
They had to baptize her at Sea World.

How can you tell your girlfriend is really fat?
She sat on a quarter and squeezed a booger out of George Washington's nose.

How can you tell your girlfriend is really fat?
Her butt looks like two pigs fighting over a pack of Milk Duds.

How can you tell your girlfriend is really fat?
She eats biscuits like they're Tic-Tacs.

How can you tell your girlfriend is really fat?
Her blood type is Ragu.

How can you tell your girlfriend is really ugly?
She has to trick-or-treat over the phone.

THE BEST SIMPLY DISGUSTING JOKES

What's the difference between a nail and your wife?
You don't need a hammer to pound your wife.

Why are gay necrophiliacs so pathetic?
Their goal in life is a dead end.

One day a twelve-year-old boy walks into a brothel, dragging a dead frog behind him.

The Madam asks, "Can I help you son?"

He replies, "Yes, I'd like a girl for the night."

She says, "I'm afraid you're too young for one of my girls."

So he gets out his wallet and gives her $200. The surprised madam says, "She'll be waiting for you upstairs."

"Not so fast," the boy adds. "The girl also has to have active herpes."

The madam protests, "But all my girls are clean."

Out comes the wallet again and he gives her another $200.

"O.K.," the madam says, "I'll have someone for you in ten minutes."

A few minutes later, the boy walks up the stairs dragging his dead frog. About thirty minutes later, he come back down the stairs, a big grin on his face, still dragging the frog.

By now the madam is curious. She asks, "Why did you come in here with a dead frog asking for a girl with herpes?"

"Well, it's like this," he says. "When I get home tonight, I'll fuck the babysitter and she'll get it. Then when my parents get home, my dad will drive her home and on the way they'll stop and have sex, so he'll get it. Later, when dad fucks mom, she'll get it. And about 9:30 tomorrow morning, the milkman will come around, fuck my mother, and *he'll* get it—and he's the bastard who killed my frog!"

Did you hear about the guy who was into sadism, bestiality and necrophilia?
He gave it up. It was beating a dead horse.

How do you know that a female bartender is pissed off with you?
There's a string hanging out of your bloody Mary.

What's green and eats nuts?
Herpes!

How do you recycle a used tampon?
As a tea-bag for vampires.

What's the best thing about having sex with a ten-year-old?
You can pretend she's five.

What's the best thing about having sex with a five-year-old?
When you hear her pelvis break.

What's the worst thing about having sex with a five-year-old?
When she says she's had better.

Carl and Vera were out walking by a lake when they saw a windsurfer zipping along just offshore. Suddenly, the surfer fell into the water and disappeared below the surface. Vera shouted, "Carl, you've got to dive in and save him."

Carl was reluctant, but Vera finally persuaded him to strip to his shorts and dive in. After several tries, he finally located a body on the bottom and dragged him to shore.

Vera said, "Quick, give him CPR."

Carl grimaced, blew once into the guy's mouth, then stood up, wretching and coughing. "God!" he swore. "This guy's got horrible breath."

Vera took a look at the man, then said, "No, wonder. We've got the wrong guy. This one's wearing skates!"

Why do tampons have strings?
So crabs can bungee-jump.

How do you make a woman scream twice?
Fuck her up the ass, then wipe it on the curtain.

What's the worst thing about having a heart/lung transplant?
Coughing up someone else's phlegm.

"Mommy, Mommy, Grandpa's going out!"
"Then put some more gasoline on him."

What's grosser than gross?
When a girl is giving you a blow job in the back seat of a car and someone crashes into you.
What's grosser than that?
When somebody slaps her on the back.

"Honey, I think the twins got into the rat poison."
"That's okay—they'll crawl under the house to die."

What's the definition of a bad day?
Going upstairs to change out of your wedding dress and finding blood on your panties.

The little girl was in trouble for wetting herself during class. "Why didn't you put your hand up?" asked the teacher.

"I did," the little girl replied, "but it kept running out."

How did the necrophiliac have his way with women?
He showed up and knocked them dead.

What's the advantage of being a cannibal and an abortionist?
You don't have to go out for lunch.

How can you tell a kid is Somalian?
His pet's a tapeworm.

What's a Somalian circumcision?
Butt-fucking your sister and having her tapeworm bite off the head.

What's printed on a necrophiliac's towels?
His and Hearse.

How does a necrophiliac sign his love letters?
"Eventually yours."

How can you tell if a pervert is a pedophiliac?
Instead of syphilis, he gets diaper rash.

How can you tell a gay pedophiliac?
He's always got his prick in the baby-shitter.

How does a necrophiliac beat the summer heat?
He goes down to the morgue and has a cold one.

Why do women have legs?
So you don't have to drag them into the bathroom to douche after you fuck them.

How is spreading fertilizer and spreading the cheeks of your ass alike?
You get the same smell from either one.

How can you tell you're in Somalia?
You throw up, and there are 20 people with straws lined up behind you.

How can you tell a woman won't win the Mother of the Year award?
She dips her baby's rectal thermometer in Ben-Gay.

What's the best way to discourage smoking?
Carry a water pistol filled with gasoline.

What's the best thing about having a homeless shelter in your neighborhood?
It keeps the flies away from your place.

What's grosser than gross?
When you dream of eating chocolate pudding and wake up with a spoon up your butt.

What's grosser than gross?
Siamese twins connected at the butt—when one farts, the other blows up.

How can you tell your kid is in a tough school?
They do abortions in biology class.

How does an Iraqi woman know her daughter has her period?
When her son tastes funny.

What do men like on pie but not on pussy?
Crust.

How can you tell your date's a pig?
You eat her pussy and get trichinosis.

How can you tell your date's a pig?
Two vultures are circling her pussy.

How can you tell your date's a pig?
A fly lands on her cunt and vomits.

What's the difference between sad and sick?
Sad is when your wife tells you she found your son smoking; sick is when it's because you set him on fire.

Why did the Polish girl put ice between her legs?
To keep the crabs fresh.

How do you know your dentures need cleaning?
Bill Clinton wants to send them to Somalia.

How do you know your teeth need brushing?
When you rinse your mouth out, it looks like you're spitting Yoo-Hoo.

How can you tell your wife's got a really huge butt?
You need a mule to get to the bottom of her crack.

How can you tell your wife's got a really huge butt?
When she wipes, she gets bat guano.

How can you tell your wife's got a really huge butt?
When she bends over, you can pick mushrooms.

What does a black woman say when you ask to use the bathroom?
"Pick a corner."

What's more disgusting than a Polack who picks his nose?
One whose boogers are so big he can use them for bowling balls.

What has two gray legs and two brown legs?
An elephant with diarrhea.

What's the difference between sad and sick?
Sad is a 45-year-old man who's saved all his baby toys; sick is a 45-year-old-man who's saved all his baby diapers.

How can you tell Uncle Ralph might not be the right babysitter?
He shows up with condoms shaped like pacifiers.

How can you tell Uncle Ralph might not be the right babysitter?
He shows up at the door with a case of Vaseline.

Did you hear about the new chic store for wealthy necrophiliacs?
It's called Neimann Carcass.

"Daddy, daddy, what's a pervert?"
"Shut up and keep sucking."

What's the difference between a white abortion and a black abortion?
Black girls abort their babies after they're born.

What's black and white and red all over?
A black man fucking a white woman who's having her period.

What's more disgusting than farting in the bathtub?
Catching the bubbles with your teeth.

What's the difference between sad and sick?
Sad is having an abortion; sick is having the fetus stuffed and mounted as a souvenir.

What's the difference between sad and sick?
Sad is having your baby die; sick is giving the bones to your dog.

What's the difference between sad and sick?
Sad is when your wife dies; sick is when you advertise her body in *The Necrophiliac News.*

Why is a fur trapper like a necrophiliac?
They're both searching for dead beavers.